This

Lisa Parker comes "from wo[illegible] first generation raised outside [illegible] of the Blue Ridge...walking the line between the mountains and the cities." As the speaker of the poem "Tracing" says, loading up her car to drive back to the city from her mountain homeplace, "I have known that spastic moment of pushing away all my life..." pushing away and yet always, always looking back. For Lisa writes from the razor edge of double consciousness which is both the gift and curse of the true poet—she is here and not here, there and not there, fully present in every moment yet already absent, too, isolating it, knowing it, naming it. She exults in "every common, common thing," finding "beauty in the scratched neon of those hometown fair rides, Kmart parking lot full of wide-eyed children sweat-palming tickets...those nights at the water tower...how the sky appeared a deep navy, banked against those black hills and jutting rockface, the distant glow of the coke furnace like a red marble perched on nothing." *This Gone Place* is more than an extraordinary collection of poems; it is Lisa Parker's hard-earned, deeply felt autobiography.

LEE SMITH
On Agate Hill and *Fair and Tender Ladies*

There is everything at stake—unabashed and utterly necessary—in Lisa Parker's brilliant first book. Memory and family and the blood of the land. Have you missed real poetry? Have you wondered where it's gone? Well, here it is. This is poetry in Lisa Parker's tending hands: stunningly new, yet familiar to the heart as scripture.

HONORÉE JEFFERS
Red Clay Suite and *The Gospel of Barbecue*

What an amazing mind comes through in every poem in this collection, a rare and wonderful distinction among first books in this country which are leaning more and more towards the cerebral—with its deep and unrelenting irony and cynicism—and moving farther and farther from human experience with all its great complexities. If indeed this place of which she writes is now "gone," it is brought back to us now, through Parker's speaker, wholecloth and shining with all the beauty and truth of that place, those people. Lisa Parker is an original voice and her work in this book moves her reader back again in to the deepest recesses of the human experience, pressing us deeply down into that thing we sometimes call a "heart."

ANNE CASTON
Flying Out With the Wounded and *Judah's Lion*

this gone place

June 2018

For Will - Brother in words & all around good guy. So glad to swap with you! All Best -

Lisa J. Parker

This Gone Place

Lisa J. Parker

ISBN 978-1-934894-29-3

POETRY

Book design

EK Larken

Front cover design

James Patterson

Photos

Lisa Parker

Grateful acknowledgment is made to the following publications in which these poems, some in different versions, appeared or are forthcoming:

Southern Review – "Body & Earth," "What Is Preserved"

Parnassus: Poetry In Review – "Penitence Enough," "Snapping Beans"

The Louisville Review – "Van Gogh's *Noon Rest From Work*"

PoetLore – "Tomato Vines" (previously titled "Comes The Dawn")

Flint Hills Review – "Salvation"

The Nantahala Review – "Bloodroot," "At the Edge of the Family, I Favor Her," "Picture of Old Mountain Woman with Frail-Looking Boy"

Wind Magazine – "First Southern Love, Done Right"

Appalachian Heritage – "Inheritance," "Learning the Retelling," "The Shape of Me," "Back Home After September"

Appalachian Journal – "Tracing," "How It Is With Dad"

Potato Eyes Literary Arts Journal – "Of Wood & Flesh"

We All Live Downstream: Writings About Mountaintop Removal (MotesBooks) – "I Mark This Gone Place With Foxfire"

Poetry: An Introduction, 4th & 5th editions (Bedford/St. Martin's Press) – "Snapping Beans"

Bedford Introduction to Literature, 7th & 8th editions (Bedford/St. Martin's Press) – "Snapping Beans"

MotesBooks

Louisville, Kentucky

www.MotesBooks.com

for my family

in memory of
Clyde & Fay Whitt

contents

foreword

I've read many poems by poets in exile from home, trying to get back to their native place and people in words. It's a familiar longing, that tension of being here and wanting to be back there, and it's been a fruitful one for Southern and particularly Appalachian poets. I know it all too well.

Lisa Parker – the "child of farmers, miners," raised somewhere between "Southern Appalachian and just plain Southern" – feels that old homesickness too, but she makes it truly new in *This Gone Place*, a passionate, smart, and beautifully bittersweet first book. The fierceness of her remembering and the honesty of her writing, especially about family, are striking. A successful woman out in the modern world, she understands the complexity of yearning for the old ways and characters and landscape – hers is no simplistic sentimentality. "I'd lay me down / in that red Virginia clay," she says, adding the final twist, "if I thought it would have me." This poetry is tender but tough: it praises and laments, it sings and stings.

Her poems about coal miners in the family are particularly original: who can forget the image of the little girl leaning against her grandfather's black-lung chest, hearing "the steady huff and whistle / of his breath – a sound / like mud daubers buzzing, / encased in their tunnels of dried earth"? And her poems about 9/11, seen from the point of view of "a Southern girl gone to Manhattan," are quietly devastating: "Sycamores" and "Last and Final Psalm" deserve to be featured in every collection of poetry from that very dark time.

But no matter where Lisa Parker is, home is in her heart, and particularly its people, "the spirit of a hundred women / who inhabit me." That precious place and those much-loved kinfolk may be disappearing or gone, but they are hardly forgotten in these tenacious poems: as she writes, "At the base of it, you are / these people. At the base of it, / you are corn and tobacco, / Irish whiskey and coal dust, / sewn of the same frayed thread / and in the same ways, / loosely sewn."

"I am beholden," Lisa Parker says near the end of *This Gone Place*, using a lovely ancient verb, "to whoever might be listening." We are beholden to her for this durable collection of poetry.

Michael McFee

prologue

Gauguin's *The Vision After The Sermon*

It isn't Jacob's bent body, held up
or dragged about by the angel.
It's the wrestling, like how my kin
in all their striving toward rightfulness –
meetings in the Farmers' Co-Op basement,
Twelve Stepping their way to salvation –
it is how they explained their evils,
the drinking, the raised fists, the wandering
eyes, how they explained them to us
children, that wrestling they did
like Jacob.

It isn't those two bent holy figures.
It's the women at the left of the tree,
their white hats, dark blue dresses.
It's their bowed heads, hands
palmed together in prayer.

It's the woman in the center, watching
the scene head-on, eyes open, the vision
coming, benign and banal as wash on a river rock.
It's how she does not flinch
at the downbent bodies or the angel,
wings spread, arms tight to Jacob's
shoulder, the back of his neck.

It's how four of the women have
no faces, beige and light dun, gray
shadow where eyes would be,
where mouths would curl to whisper, to call
the Rosary and *mea culpa* to see
the staggering man.

It's how they are faceless as those babies
Grandma delivered, twins, a caul
over the firstborn's face, a sign
of second sight, though he was born
blind and his twin without breath
or cry, skin gray with what couldn't be.

And me? I'm there, behind the rounded turn
of tree trunk, nails digging the bark,
one eye on the angel, the other squeezed
tight to blur the sight of a man succumbing,
the wrestling done, his back curved,
his face stricken, maybe,
or euphoric.

i

Inheritance

I am from women whose wombs rained babies,
whose breasts hung useless
without hungry children's mouths,
from a grandmother who worked herbal remedies
over childhood ailments, wrapped my body
in poultices of wild onion, beef tallow and mayapple root,
drank with me the foul treebark teas
that drew fever and congestion from the body.
I am from a mother whose Cherokee cheekbones
eluded me, whose womb pushed me into the light
of January sun, of smalltown South - the first
generation raised outside the hollers of the Blue Ridge.
I am a voice blurring dialects
of Southern Appalachian and just plain Southern,
walking the lines between the mountains
and the cities, afraid of the fringe
I inhabit, afraid to admit
that I come from the spirit of a hundred women
who inhabit me, who are with me
in these cities, in these universities,
and who sing beneath my skin,
Look away, Look away.

Snapping Beans

for Fay Whitt

I snapped beans into the silver bowl
that sat on the splintering slats
of the porchswing between my grandma and me.
I was home for the weekend,
from school, from the North.
Grandma hummed "What A Friend We Have In Jesus"
as the sun rose, pushing its pink spikes
through the slant of cornstalks,
through the fly-eyed mesh of the screen.
We didn't speak until the sun overcame
the feathered tips of the cornfield
and Grandma stopped humming. I could feel
the soft gray of her stare
against the side of my face
when she asked, *How's school a-goin?*
I wanted to tell her about my classes,
the revelations by book and lecture
as real as any shout of faith,
potent as a swig of strychnine.
She reached the leather of her hand
over the bowl and cupped
my quivering chin;
the slick smooth of her palm held my face
the way she held cherry tomatoes under the spigot,
careful not to drop them,
and I wanted to tell her
about the nights I cried into the familiar
heartsick panels of the quilt she made me,
wishing myself home on the evening star.
I wanted to tell her
the evening star was a planet,
that my friends wore noserings and wrote poetry
about sex, about alcoholism, about Buddha.

I wanted to tell her
how my stomach burned acidic holes
at the thought of speaking in class,
speaking in an accent, speaking out of turn,
how I was tearing, splitting myself apart
with the slow-simmering guilt of being happy
despite it all.
I said, *School's fine.*
We snapped beans into the silver bowl between us
and when a hickory leaf, still summer green,
skidded onto the porchfront,
Grandma said,
It's funny how things blow loose like that.

Backslid North

I.

I am filled with words like drowned bodies.
Just beneath the water's surface, they bloat
indignantly. I see their watchful eyes -
pine and mud-colored like mine.
I hear the soft gurgle I've reduced them to.

II.

Granddaddy told me once,
Don't get above your raising.
I call him often to practice my self,
to remember that I am all about
holler and *giggin*, *heared tell of* and *sigodlin*.

I am taking steps.
I talk of craving pork rinds.
I drawl hard.
I write this poem out of spite.

III.

I am full of poems that lie
the language right out of me.
I've whitewashed my South Appalachian
to an *understandable* hue, put those *regional* words
in jars with lace lids and waited, breath held,
for the scholarly nods. That approval
is almost enough to tolerate knowing
that between what I *am* and what I *write*,
something is rotting.

Penitence Enough

If I thought it was penitence enough
for turning my back,
for this fraudulence I wear
like a pond film over my skin,
I'd return home,
and lay deep
in that Old Dominion soil.
I'd pull the hollyhocks close,
sprout pennyroyal – pungent mint
and purple bloom – from my teeth,
my eyes full of nothing
but the backs of Blue Ridge steeps,
ears tipped with corn tassels
and calamus root and nothing
but the roll of the Shenandoah,
the ring of a banjo carried down
on mountain wind.
I would stand still and long
as August heat
till the kudzu took me over,
wound itself through me,
anchored me to that land
I can still see under my nails
after months of scrubbing.
I'd press my face to the cool damp
of the cannery walls,
my knees against the porch boards.
I'd open veins and spill
against the sycamore roots,
give myself over,
give myself back,
and lay me down
in that red Virginia clay -
if I thought it would have me.

Body And Earth

for Clyde Whitt

When I was small, I slept
in Granddaddy's arms, my head
against his chest, dozing
to the rhythmic wheezing
my mama called Black Lung.

He muscled his pickaxe and shovel
into the black guts of the mountains
for twenty-five years, stooped ten inches
beneath the safety timbers
that held the earth.

We sit on the porchswing,
whittling twigs into smaller twigs
while Grandma hums "Over In The Gloryland,"
dips old cornshucks into a mason jar of water,
soaking out the dry age, their brittle edges softening.
She bends them, pliant and fresh again with water,
twisting them into bright, yellow dolls.

I look at Granddaddy's fingers, knuckled deep and bent
around his knife, lean against the sagging
point of his shoulder
and listen to the steady huff and whistle
of his breath – a sound
like mud daubers buzzing,
encased in their tunnels of dried earth.

Fear And A Country Breakfast

Chicken feed
swirls crazy in autumn wind,
buckshot of cornseed and gravel
in my eyes.
Grandma's feet,
heavy in plastic-soled slippers,
crunch on feed and pebbles.
Her pastel flowered robe
brushes the ground,
swings into a squall of feathers.
My fingers,
nails full of hickory bark
from my desperate tree-clutch,
shove against my eardrums,
against the final snap –
like a maple twig in deep winter.
Grandma yawns her way
to the shed,
white feathers dangling from her hand –
twitching, still clucking insanely,
one finger around the axe handle, two,
one more yawn on the downswing.
After the dull thump of the axe,
the scratching claws
run over feed and gravel,
and where I run,
the spastic death legs
point, propel the blood-
soaked body in a staggering
chase, so close
to dancing, these
intricate circles
toward each other,
and always

Grandma kicks the head
to the cats
before I can see
if the eyes follow me.

First Southern Love, Done Right

First Southern love, when it's with the raised-right,
still boy enough not to wanna wait,
man enough to do it right,
that's the kind not suited to backseats.
No vinyl for this sweet zinnia,
no Lynrd Skynrd on the stereo or radio commercials
for A&P and Booth Feed; not when she can have
the sway and sway of a wheatfield
or the quiet of a hayloft. Mountains and valleys
can sneak her into coves of wild fieldgrass,
or overhangs of tulip poplars and sycamores
that blow across her skin and cool the sweat
where it stands.

It's not about, *I'll call you some time.*
It's about the rounded rock he'll pull,
smooth and cold from the riverbed, and wrap
in cattail fluff to hold against her
until the bleeding stops.
When it's right, he won't sit too close in church
or blush in front of her daddy.
They'll wait, on slow simmer, until they can put
a valley or two between themselves and everyone,
find sun against their skin,
an audience of bluejays and cardinals,
and a river to swim in when being naked
is the only way to be.

Salvation

for Lee

I knelt before the pews and washed
those knobbed, curling feet of old women
because Grandma said,
Hit's the way o' the Lord.
Grandma called it my fire,
that used to burn outward,
move over my skin,
make me dance and shout out
words I didn't know, the fire
that climbed through my throat
in bursts of bluegrass gospel,
sent me reeling toward the waters of the Levisa River
and the outstretched arms of Reverend Spiers,
water that lapped at my ankles, my calves,
my thighs, in sweet Jesus ecstasy
as he laid me back into the murky salvation
and all the week's cornsilk cigarettes
smoked behind the springhouse,
the unclean thoughts about Harlan Hess,
all of it washed away
down the current
that ran black and gritty
with coal dust from the mines.

We sat near the front pews, near enough
to hear the rattling in those boxes,
smell the bread and sweet yeast of wine
beneath the linen shroud that quaked
with each pound of the preacher's veiny fist;
the splintering pews, the smell of people
sitting too close, all of it built
into the frenzy whose only relief

was the cool water and the sureness
of knowing I would be saved.

Grandma cried, arms above her head,
eyes shut tight, squeezing salty praise
and exaltation that burned her
the way my fire burned me.
Even underwater, I could hear her shouting,
Yes, Lord, bless her!
and when I emerged onto the river bank,
covering breasts I didn't yet have, she sat me
beneath the pawpaw trees, her hands
deep in my hair, braiding the tangled brown
as my dress dried
and pulled away from my skin.

Failing Out of College

for Silas

She wasn't kidding herself, meant what she was saying,
most of it, even if the bile rose each time she laughed,
told her friends *Too damned expensive –*
who needs the debt?
And anyway, who decided there was nothing more
to say about the South in poetry hadn't been said before?
She didn't pay for them to tell her holler wasn't a real word,
for some snot-nosed Ohioan to say, *Jesus, another black*
lung poem
and her sitting there quiet like she didn't really
lose him to it,
like she hadn't spent her life watching him spit his lungs
out on the ground like some ordinary thing. And that slow,
electric buzz in her fingers, the humming in her ears
to look at them, *colleagues*, knowing not one of them
had ever sat up all night, thanking Jesus
for that miner's pension,
for the funeral home with its air conditioning
and quiet, appropriate music, no wailing, no great aunts
seized in tongues because it was *public*, and him, laid out
dignified in a suit, in a pillowy coffin, no shroud, no
body stiff on the table in their living room, parts bent
and not touching where they ought to, eyes she knew
were never fully closed beneath those nickels.
These people didn't know shit.

There was beauty in the scratched neon
of those hometown fair rides, Kmart parking lot
full of wide-eyed children sweat-palming tickets,
teenagers behind the House of Horrors, kissing sloppily,
clutching each other with fervor only the young
and desperate can attain. She knew
those nights at the water tower, perched high enough

on the catwalk to see most of the town, how the sky
appeared a deep navy, banked against those black hills
and jutting rockface, the distant glow of the coke furnace
like a red marble perched on nothing.
That was beautiful.

And there would be something beautiful
in going back to her family's home, her mama
in the kitchen cooking to Paula Deen on the t.v.,
feeding her spoonfuls of something new,
exotic but still Southern,
and later, propping herself against the headboard
to fill out applications,
to turn, finally, to that journal, and write
and write
and write
every little thing that passes that window,
every finch on the poplar, every mantis on the sill,
every common, common thing.

Of Wood And Flesh

for Dad

In winter, the dry gray
cracks across your knuckles
making them bleed pretty red
down the axe handle.
You show me what a poplar knot looks like
from the inside
split open.
I'm not afraid to hold the wedge for you.
I would give my fingers easily.
I like the ache in my shoulders,
the kindling bruises across my knees.
I'm like you,
smelling the oaks, pines, cedars;
I know them blind.
Mama says of all your daughters,
I am the closest you got
to a son.
You wink at me over
our piles of chopped hickory.
We share coffee,
sit flannel to flannel,
father and daughter
on the chopping block.

Anomaly

A month of oddities in weather
since the winter solstice moon
when it lay so heavy and close on the tips
of hickory and dogwood I thought
to put down my camera and not molest it
for fear it would raise itself high again
and out of reach.

It is mid-January already and the wind tears
the branches to the ground, but so mild
the temperature, I sit with only a flannel on,
press my back against the scratch
and smooth of cherry bark.
It is easy to imagine the violence to skin and bone
if the sun ducked too long behind the rushing clouds
and plunged the air back out over the pond water,
only now just thawing where today's sun and warmth
comb the ditch water in cracking strands across
the thin crystal, so young and shallow yet
in this strange winter.

Second Hand

for Gene, Raymond, and James

Fourteen years of classical piano
just so I could turn these well-trained fingers
to the wire strangeness of a guitar I bought
secondhand, my fumbling attempt to strum and twang,
to tie myself beyond the blood and bone we share
to great uncles and aunts, to the mountains
and hollers I longed to claim.

Granddaddy insisted I learn real music,
fancy music like Chopin, Rachmaninoff.
But I see how his eyes widen
when I sit between his brothers, singing
the mountain ballads and old time gospel.
When I sing, *Ruby Are You Mad At Your Man*,
and Uncle Gene and I sing harmony on old
Stanley Brothers tunes, Granddaddy sits,
his head bowed, listening, concentration so complete
it near to closes my throat.

We put up the guitars and he sits beside me,
asks about my piano music, but takes my hand as we talk,
runs his thumb over the grooved calluses
on the tips of my fingers.

Tomato Vines

Huddled by the woodstove,
your flannel hangs faded
over sagging shoulders.
The nights come earlier now,
spreading with less pink over the edges
of cornfields and you wander the house,
room to room, your eyes scanning
floor to ceiling. I have seen you
run your hands against the paneling,
checking the soundness
though you built these walls yourself;
a miner's habit, scrutinizing the strength
of what holds the weight above you.

Fifty years beyond the shafts at the RedJacket Mine,
you still crouch, eyes wide and searching
the dawn that creeps over the backs
of the cedars, and when it comes,
you stand again, wander the garden
and touch the tomato vines where morning dew
catches the first light across their laden leaves.

Autumn

It is about preparedness,
about making it through the winter,
and so I have always thought I would write
about the dramatics of the season; the hunts,
shotgun shells lying bright against soggy leaves,
hogs splayed, hollowed out
and hanging from the maples.
I have always craved that fine art of survival,
so honed in my grandfather, my uncles, so graceful
in their sure strides into the woods, their hands
as agile canning jars of pickled corn as they are
drawing the strong swipes of their knives over deer.

But I find myself going back to those cool days
I feigned illness to bypass school, to lie in the backseat
of the red stationwagon, scratchy carpet against
the fingertips of the hand I flopped dramatically
to the floor, my mother driving me
to Grandma's house, not buying the act,
not calling me on it either.

If Granddaddy grew something unruly in me,
those women tempered it with long, Fall afternoons,
out on the swaying wood of the porchswing,
beneath the quilt of Biblical panels, Moses
and the tablets, his face unveiled and radiant as sun,
and Grandma's foot always gently pushing
while she peeled potatoes into a kitchen pail
and I counted leaves as they ticked off the limbs
of great oaks whose branches touched the roof,
the side of the porch, dipping against the frame of house
as if holding it there, pressing it all to stillness.

ii

Dreaming Granddaddy

A child, I dreamed you as those black and whites
in Grandma's family album, your miner's lamp
like a third eye perched at the brim of your hat,
your skin black with coal dust you still bring up
with solid coughs. I dreamed you tall
before the mines bent you to the curve
of twenty-five years' pickaxe and shovel weight
and the black rock you hefted onto carts and belts.

Lately, I've dreamed you
as part of the mountains – all six feet of you
stuffed into a coal seam, the way you said
you shoved cartridges of powder
into an auger-drilled hole, packed it good
and tight with the tamper and lit the fuse.
Sleep hinges on that moment of soundlessness.

I wait for the shift of slate,
the slipping face of coal walls
that signal the shaft dwellers to come,
shovels in hand, and lift the broken pieces
onto carts to be dragged toward the light
of surface and grass.

Deluge

Watermelons burst, split
green and white rind,
ripe flesh exploding with rain,
oversaturated, pink meat dries,
a rubbery sheen in the sun.

Foxes pounce in the crossfield
on mice celebrating the abundance
in hayrolls that can't be put up
until they dry out – one damp patch
would bring it down, barn and all,
in spontaneous flame. They think this
a gift, these mice, ferreting their pieces
of berry and nuts, their young.
Foxtails go skyward, red flashes
through fieldgrass and goldenrod.

Tobacco fields bend, leaves rotting,
blue mold laying heavy on them,
laying leaves to a fine fuzz,
laying them to waste.

As children, we sang a special prayer
for rain, for the blessing of water
to field, row of corn, bean and potato.
For this overabundance,
we have no song.

At Ashby Gap, Fourth Grade

LeeAnn sits beneath the toothed leaves
of a spreading chinquapin tree, picking up
spiny nuts with one hand, two fingers,
bloody-tipped already, pull back
the vest pockets on her shirt. She slips
the terrible spiked things into each pocket
and I ask what she's doing.
There is a white ring around her mouth
and her dark hair splays in sweaty streaks
against her neck. *I ain't gonna be the only one*
in class without a necklace.
My granny showed me this.

When her pockets are full, she presses
three fingers inside to make room
for just one more handful.
Look how many.
Later, when she empties the pockets
into a small, ceramic bowl, I watch
her tiny breasts leak slow blood against
her tee shirt where the brambles dug in.
The nuts lie bunched together,
their spikes meshed and tangled,
the tiniest red on an occasional tip.

She will boil them free of their spikes,
string them with a needle and fishing line
she found dangling on a low branch
of skeletal sycamore, bleached white
and groping at the stream's edge.
She will wear the necklace to school,
finger the smooth round of each nut on the bus ride.
The preppies in their Izod and Jordache
will laugh at her, ask her if she uses her necklace
to fish with in the evenings.

At recess, she will sit behind the concrete piping
at the edge of the back field
and eat each nut slowly,
swearing their sweetness to the still, September air.

Breaking Fever

for Grandma

I sipped bitter tea of peachtree bark
and branch water for your story
about how to cut the limb
the right way:
You run your knife up the limb
to treat a fever; for chills and the like,
you run it down the limb,
take the shavings and steep them twenty minutes.
When you grated ginger root into bowls
of applesauce, I ate past nausea
to hear at each swallow, *Look how strong my girl is.*

Your fingers, with their Cherokee tan, worked
over my body, rubbing my feet to draw
the fever down. In moments of rest,
your hands lay against mine, paling
my own Irish tint to a ghostlier white. You said,
We're the same blood, child.
Dark nor fair don't make a bit of difference.

When my stomach turned toward fever, you brought
the kitchen pail to hold my head over.
You tossed the remnants of a morning's work of herbs
into the woods and held the pail into the cold,
rushing water of the branch, never hinting
disgust, no weariness at the thought of gathering
the herbs again, steeping the bark, finding the story
to tell while I sipped and we waited
for my body's revolt or the brief respite of sleep.
When the fever broke, you said,
That's the bark takin hold. See?
Mountain women carry the earth
close to their bodies.

You propped me against you, fed me
ice chips, passing them across my lips
with your fingers,
not wanting the metal spoon
between us.

Down Home

for Beth

Down home they'd have forced ipecac
down your throat — conscious or not —
made dashes to the root cellar,
air heavy with yarrowroot, boiling slippery elm
and juniper berries and the men searching the holler
for the preacher, spitting great nervous wads of tobacco.
They'd have covered you in cheesecloth
poultices to bring you around,
and when the last remedies failed,
they'd have given over
to raw wailing against the mountains.

Down home they'd have moved your body
onto a shawled table, covered your eyes
with shiny nickels, your body
with a hand-stitched shroud
and I'd have been able to see you, hold
the shell of you against me
no matter how late I was.

At Dawn on a Hunting Morning

His Winchester 12-gauge leans
against kitchen wall paneling,
old linoleum crackles rhythmically under Granddaddy's
foot,
tapping unconsciously to *Barbara Ellen*
on the kitchen radio,
static gets louder or lesser depending
where Grandma stands, where she moves
from cast iron skillets
to refrigerator, back again.
He pours milk into his coffee without looking,
pours the coffee from cup to saucer beneath,
the green and white Corel pattern covered over,
edges showing as he tilts the saucer, lifts
to just beneath his mouth, blowing
small ripples across it before drinking.

She hums a hymn separate from the mountain voices
on the radio and I realize *that* is what he keeps rhythm to
as he stares out the frosted window, one eye
a scarred blue, fixed on something near the wood's edge
or the shed or nothing I would see
even if I looked.

Oncology Unit: Fauquier Hospital

His arm is wrapped in the sheet,
hand angled toward his chin, posturing
even in this sedated sleep.
It is a broken wing he clutches to him,
an arm withered now, sinking into itself,
into the holes where cancer bores into bone
and cartilage. I want to touch it,
to brush down the sweat-strewn hairs
like feathers turned the wrong way.

My aunt circles the bed, watching
the labored breaths that heave noisily
from his mouth, bottom lip bouncing,
folding itself in and out with each draw
of oxygen, each gulp toward the browning lungs
where all this started.

My aunt circles the bed, watching
the nurses take his temperature, change
his I.V. bags. She has posted a sign
above the bed in bright red marker:
DO NOT MOVE RIGHT ARM!
Two nurses ignored the sign, didn't see it,
thought they knew better than this woman,
crazed with lack of sleep and pacing and coffee.
They tried to straighten it, tried to pry it
from its atrophied home against his chest.
He cried then, from his sleep, from the place
the drugs held him, cried loudly and without restraint
and so much like his grandbabies had cried
in the lobby of that very hospital
that we all gasped and turned our heads from it.

I heard my aunt growl then, low and almost inaudible

against the beeping of IV regulators, oxygen hissing.
I heard the plastic creaking of the mattress behind me,
knew she was leaning across it toward those women,
her voice, deep and raspy as she said,
You will not touch him again.

What Is Preserved

What I remember most about that night
is how, a few minutes after the call, she came,
my grandmother, to my bedroom holding a hair pick
outstretched toward me.

I cain't do it.

In the bathroom, her thin hair gave
easily under the combing
and I fluffed the back, teased it for body.
I felt her shoulder shaking against the hand I rested there,
looked up to the mirror and watched her eyes giving way.
The backward glance she refused me
held us still and silent, my hand poised
above her head. She braced her hands
against the sink, gripped the formica
til her fingernails blanched.
She knew not to look back at me
just as she knew not to look at her son
that night, face bloated with chemo, one arm
wrapped and posturing toward his neck,
a sterile, broken thing. She knew well
the lesson of Lot's wife,
the price of looking back.

I did not hold her then,
but combed her hair into submission, watched
her face smooth out again, the tears slowing,
stopping. She sniffed hard, once,
looking, finally, into my face in the mirror and said,
Now spray it so it'll keep,
and I covered her face with my hand,
spraying her hair into place, touching
her forehead lightly,
shielding her eyes.

When I Realized My Mother Couldn't Swim

I said, *I would save you if you fell off the boat.*
I envisioned myself pulling you from the Shenandoah's
muddy brown and rushing current, pulling you
to the boat's edge or the cattailed shore. You said,
If I fell over, you would leave me.
You are too small and I am too big.

Years since, I have dreamed slow motion dreams,
the kind I can't wake from in time to stop
my body's shaking or the sweat that eases
into the cotton sheets, sour and binding.
It's not your falling into that muddy water,
but the way the water clears
when I lock my legs around your waist,
expel the last breath toward the surface;
I see the last shake of your head,
the half moons on my thighs, where you dig your nails
to pry me off, to send me to the surface, to wake
wet and cold and in the dark.

How It Is With Dad

We record our history in fishing trips,
mark our relationship by the steady row
and drift of our boat on the James River. Our story
is dogeared like pages of a book you want to remember
by talk that comes easily over a ten-pound test
and graphite rod and the shared plea to reel in
a channel cat or large-mouthed bass. We share
a ham sandwich and I study the impression
of your teeth in the bread, the places where our bites
overlap in the stack of meat and lettuce. I could tell you
I know without looking the angle of your arm
when you cast,
but we share a respect for water and sun and silence.

When I cast my line close to the shore without snagging
the hanging limbs of willows and shore oaks,
you say, *That a girl.*

November Ground

I.

My cousin lay under the stiff
white sheets in that hospital bed
and died after two days
of coma, of tubes and swelling.
Our family waited for the miracle we were due.
She had been saved,
washed in the blood of the lamb,
in the water that took her over
with hardly a drop lost
over the edges of the baptismal.
She rededicated her faith twice,
prayed against the regimen
of blue and red pills, the word manic,
the voices in her head that said
FAT HOG
until she weighed 80 pounds
and swallowed a pill
for each pound.
Dead, a few days
before Thanksgiving.

II.

Hogs should be slaughtered
when they weigh between 180 and 240 pounds.

III.

In the hills,
November is the month of the slaughter.
Hogs roam the mountains,
gorging themselves on acorns and roots

until Granddaddy runs them
down the holler into pens he's made
from old timber and chickenwire.
He fires his .410 into the air
to scare them down the mountain
and yells, *Hogs a-coming!*
Get off'n the hill!

Those hogs would trample us to death
if they got the chance.

IV.

The day of the funeral,
my car ran out of gas,
and I walked the gravel road
to a country store with one gas pump,
an old man who said
I could have as much gas
as I could carry, pay him
on my way back through.
He followed me out to the pump.
I heared about your cousin. Law, that's a shame.
Still, hit ain't for us to decide our own fate.
Hit's an abomination
in His eyes.

Gas cans pulled my arms
toward the ground as I walked
away from the store, my knuckles
trying to hold the cans steady, trying
not to spill. I looked back
at the old man standing,
swallowed up by the shadow of a sign
that hung on the storefront behind him.
It said:
AT THE END – YOU MEET GOD.

V.

The blunt side meets its mark
between the eyes, one swing
of Granddaddy's axe, one hog
at a time.

Once, when we were small
and watched the slaughter
on a dare from older cousins,
she sobbed each hog as they dropped.
When Granddaddy heard her,
he came across the field, still holding
the axe in the giant bend of his hand
and her eyes were wide as half dollars
when he knelt down in front of her
and said, *They's no other way.*
Besides, they wasn't hurtin, honey,
they never even seed it comin.

VI.

I watch my uncles pour
great tubs of scalding water
over the hog's body,
kneel beside its great head
and the steam is still
rising, warming my hands
as I run the edge of the knife
over its neck, scraping the coarse hair
that falls like a hundred pine needles
against my bloodied boots.
When it is bald, we hang it
by its hind legs, a heavy stick
between the legbone and hamstring
exposed with two quick cuts.
My uncles heft the stick between

the forks of two trees and I
am eye level with the smooth belly.
There is no divine intervention.
I am not Abraham and God doesn't tell me
to put down my knife.
With one long drag of the blade,
I open it to spill against the cold,
November ground.
There is no cry now to bear witness,
no shout of protest or message
by way of a cold wind.
Nothing but the sucking sound I imagine
coming from the hard earth as it draws in
the hog's blood. I imagine the potatoes,
deep in the frozen dirt, sprouting eyes
against this warm invasion
and I want to tell the old man at the country store:
At the end,
it is *all* an abomination.

At the Edge of the Family, I Favor Her

for Lindsay Paige

Because she is always covering something,
  her body with tattoos and piercings, her mouth
when she laughs, her ears when she thinks no one
  is watching and she aches for silence outside
this noisy family.
  Because I have seen her sway, eyes closed,
in the back lawn to Grandma's radio leaking country
  classics
  out the kitchen window, propped open to air the heat,
because she would deny dancing to that music,
  adamantly, deny dancing at all, moving her body in a
  fashion
so predictable to music so *hick*, so *us*.
  Because she sits close to me at these family functions,
her long fingers rubbing nervously against each other,
  stilling when I lace them between my own.
Because she is seventeen and it has somehow come to her
  that she is a lesser version of this swarm
of well-meaning, judging people.

  I hold her close to me when she allows it,
trace the butterfly inked into the back of her neck,
  tell her she is lovely, unique, tell her
I have seen her dance, barefoot in the summer grass,
  that the sway of her hips, her arms above her head
are so graceful, she is fine and white as the egrets
  we watched together at the pond's edge
when she was small enough for my lap. I tell her
  she is such a sight to behold
I cannot hear the music.

Learning the Retelling

I know his stories;
the coon hunts, the woman who fed him
a pail full of cornbread wrapped in linen
when he walked 50 miles to West Virginia
and stopped before her house to ask food for work.
The stories come more frequently now
from his chair beside the heat stove.
He knows I will remember them all,
but he speaks again to be sure I get it in the retelling,
how the mines could blow at any time if coal dust built,
how he pulled the body of a man from beneath the rocks
and saw his eye sitting halfway down his cheek.
It is important, these details.

There is no poetry to pretty up
that man's face, or my grandfather's,
hungry in youth, still aching against it
all these years later.

The Falling Toward You

I have never feared the spirits
nor have I much acknowledged them
beyond their appearance in my features,
their contribution to temper and stubbornness.
But how hard it has been today
not to call out to you directly, Beth,
when the sun falls through the trees
on the places we sat and played as children
and I am sure it falls in the same patterns,
warms the soil and mulch, ready for our nimble fingers
to dig the day's catch of root and onion grass.

It is out of stubbornness that I refuse you most days.
How hard it is still, nearly five years gone,
to think of you with the sun
thick in your hair, to think of those days
we played happily by Granddaddy's garden.
How hard it is to question the honesty of that, the truth
about what lay against that happiness,
just beneath it, maybe.
So I will lay the questions aside today.
I will feel you pass against my shoulders.
I won't shudder, but lean toward you,
into the wind, lean until I am falling
against this sun-crisped fieldgrass, until
the unyielding ground rushes against me,
leaves me breathless,
reaching.

Picture of Old Mountain Woman with Frail-Looking Boy

I.

She swore by the prickly-ash trees
for their easy cure of tooth ache,
showed him the soft, translucent dots
on leaves she ran across the back of his hand,
as if touching them would commit them
to his memory, would guarantee the passing
from her generation to his.

II.

The explosions were like shotgun fire,
wrecking the silence of dire winter
and he pressed himself to her side, scratch
of wool that she held him against, though one hand
pressed flat to his back, pushed him forward
toward the destruction, the other hand,
waxy smooth fingers tracing the veins in his palm
as she told him how when sap rose in maples
and poplars, it sometimes froze, exploding
the tree, imbedding splinters in oaks nearby.

III.

Her mind is old now, one tree blending
into the next and he takes his place
at her side, reminds her which leaves or bark
bring down fever, which ones a cough.
But those days will always be
about his easy flinching
and the way she pushed him with sure hands
over ground covered in pieces of wood, things
brought down from the inside.

Looking For Bernard

More than a half century after his death,
I walked the cemetery with Grandma,
looking for her baby's grave –
unmarked except for a stone
that was long gone, eroded
by rains and snows and leaves.
It should be near this oak tree.
But she couldn't remember which direction,
and the heat bore down on us, the air
holding down the leaves to a weak
and occasional breeze, even there,
on the top of that mountain.

I went to her, and she said,
I ain't sure where it is,
I just ain't sure.

She studied every rock marker,
bending slowly over them,
running her fingers over their tops,
laying, one by one, the artificial flowers
against strange stones.

What Slips From the Body

At the back of MacGregor's field
where we tipped them on full-mooned nights,
a great Holstein lay
bloating into July heat.
We found her with our noses first,
the smell of decay slipping through the fingers
I clamped over my mouth to hold back the retch.

This was the smell of pond bottom dwellers;
those snapping turtles that surfaced
to dare us into the murk, to dip our toes
beneath what we could see.

We circled the cow, noses pinched, surveying
the way the fur matted with something
slick and clear around the tail and eyes.
Standing close to the belly we could hear
scratching sounds. Something pushed
against the brick brown fur, moved it
in subtle twitches. J.B. Rodgers poked the belly
with his walking stick, the tip
slipped easily past fur and skin that buckled
and pulled apart in the heat. He cried out,
jumped back, the stick fell from his hand, the tip
out of the cow. The air rushed from the hole,
pushed past the hand I still held clamped over
my face and I choked
on the sour hot of it.

Before I turned to run, the possum
crawled out the back end of the cow,
covered in the shiny grease
that colored it darker gray.
The rat-like tail was the last thing I saw, slipping

from the cow's body
with a wet, slick sound,
leaving its trail on the summer-scorched grass.

Tracing

It is July and I am home again
from the city, walking the backyard
to trace those places where grass refuses
to grow, the places where my feet dug in
toes and heels, a child, looking for the ground's firm
grip, the traction to push me ahead of my cousins
in foot races and games of tag.

The wild raspberry vines rush over
the fence and hang like hair
across the shoulders of chainlink. Mama says,
There's poison sumac mixed in.
Mind you don't reach into it.
She is on the back porch,
watching me. She tells me
they took down the swingset, finally,
because it rusted and pieces broke off
jagged and waited to be stepped on.
Beneath that same ground of rust and wild weeds,
my dog Jessie is buried.

I run my fingers over the clumps of berries,
take only the ones that fall easily into my hand
from the sticky, orange swords they have sheathed
through these days of sun and occasional rain.
Later, we make jam and pies
and she reminds me how to melt the paraffin
for the lids, how much sugar to add
for the pies, how much salt for the crust.
When the kitchen is steaming with our work, she wipes
the sweat from my face with a damp kitchen cloth,
sings some old Southern gospel, nods her head
when I remember some of the words,
sing high harmony with her.

In the morning, my car is packed full
with rolls of paper towels, boxes of macaroni,
things she pulled from the pantry
and rushed into my arms, waving my protests away
with a gentle hand, a push toward the car.
The box on the passenger-side floor holds jars of jam
and a raspberry pie, warm enough still
to sprinkle the plastic wrap with beads.
She leans in my window, rushes a kiss against my lips,
too quick for me to return the affection, her hands
moving to hold my face tightly for only a moment,
not long enough for me
to cover her hands with my own,
my hands left dangling mid-air as she reaches across me,
turns the ignition for me, steps back.
Go on now. Get going.
I watch her in the rearview mirror, at the end
of the driveway, pumping on tiptoes,
waving wildly, her movements unwieldy, frantic
in her effort to keep from crying.

I have known that spastic movement of pushing away
for all my life, known the truth of tears she will cry
when I am out of sight. I want to be offended
at this rushing, her flighty dance, always
one step from my reach, never still enough
to hold firmly against me nor quiet enough to hear
my declarations of love, of homesickness. But I know
she is remembering the singing in that kitchen, the feel
of old pitches finding each other, thinking that maybe
in those moments of song when I am as young
as she wants me to be, my face wiped beneath her
careful cloth, that it isn't lost on either of us;
Mama with her elusive touch and quick smile,
and me, my arm out the car window, waving
until I can't see her anymore.

Sounding

(Sounding is a technique used by coalminers; they knock on the mine's ceiling and listen to see whether it is sound and safe to work under)

You are scaffolding now –
all ribs and cheekbones, point of hips.
When your breath pauses, I count the seconds –
20, 30, 40
and you gasp the air back in,
your eyes opening wide, unfocused.

I want to ask you how different this is,
this dark breathlessness. How different
from those moments you told me
you could hear the mountain ease above
and around you in the hollowed coal rooms
of the mines?

You escaped the crash and explosion of dust and gas
to raise up your family, to teach me bluegrass,
your sons how to grow a proper garden.
Now, sixty-odd years beyond those shafts
you lay on the bed we've made of this couch –
too proud to use the hospital bed
in the corner of the next room.

I take your hand, sweaty and cold,
tell you that I'm here and you slip back again
to the agonal breathing, that place
between sleep
and death
and I lay my head lightly
on your chest,

tap
          and listen

for the rumbling
          before the fall.

iii

Van Gogh's *Noon: Rest From Work*

The man in the shade of his labor
is called resting, arms folded behind his head, hat
pushed down over his eyes, an illusion of rest
but for the sheaves bound beside him,
his day's work and another day's still
beneath the head he rests on towering straw.

Child of farmers, miners, I know to look
at the feet for the truth and I find it there,
his shoes off, the edges worn down,
feet bent with years of standing,
threshing, binding, his work spelled out
plain against arches long gone, toes
curling downward, searching the earth out.

The sickles lie beside his shoes,
the curve of one blade over
the point of the other.
They are two snakes, heads
cocked back to strike or wrap their necks
one around the other.

I picture my grandfather there,
his feet curled, knobbed to the roughened
boots, the ceaseless standing.
He would be stooped,
squatting the peasant's squat,
a habit taken from those deep shafts when he moved
from one labor of soil to another.

He would want Van Gogh's easy strokes
to curve the ribs' pointed testimony
to gaunt seasons, the bend of knee
and elbow gone with arthritis.

He would want these sloping brushstrokes
of loose shirt and spiraling straw,
no sharp edges to tear clothes or skin,
no places brought together at a point, no corner.
Even the sky, crisp blue swirls verging on breeze,
so different from the mine's wet air,
everything tamped to stillness.

Open Chamber, Slide Shut

Come back, Granddaddy, back
to these woods we walked. Find me here,
back against this birch tree, this cold fog
eating the scenery to twenty-foot's depth.
I am lost in this awful mist of rain, bones
chilled to this air, fifty degrees at best,
though it's nearly June. You would call this
blackberry winter, this weather.
You would tell me, *Get off'n that ground!*
You would take this rifle, cradled against my chest,
and show me how to shoot it proper.
My pockets sag with .22 cartridges I have yet
to fire. I bought this gun for no reason
but to come to these woods in ownership of it,
to shout for you, "Remington, single shot,
bolt action, .22 long rifle" and imagine you
standing behind me, proud, your long arms molded
to mine, positioning the smooth, sheer wood
against my shoulder, helping me sight the hay bales
I can't even see now through this fog.

I watch a bead gather on the bill of my hat, swollen,
watch it fall against the long barrel in my lap, slide
to my arm, spread into nothing against flannel.
The mist swirls in a strong wind, gathers itself again,
glides its slow dance over wet leaves and black walnuts
gone to seed against the forest floor. When it lifts
enough to see my bales again, I slide the chamber open,
pull an oily smooth bullet from my shirt pocket,
lay it in, slide it closed. I prop the barrel on one knee,
squint, hold my breath. You would say,
They ain't no kick to speak of. Don't flinch.
and so I pull the trigger, feel the gentle wood
press back into my shoulder, watch the satisfying spray

of damp hay, watch it settle again over branches and moss.

I open the chamber, gold pellet ejecting into my lap,
shut it again, slide it open, click it shut, the snap
and bolt of metal gliding into metal, locking, lulling.
I want to bend my head in reverence to this.
I want to call out, *This is you, Old Man, this sound.*
I close my eyes and you are plain before me,
hunting cap pulled tight, quilted, tan jacket,
rifle in your great hand like it weighs nothing.
I slide the chamber open, slide it closed.
It is a simple thing, this missing you;
small as the music from this rifle,
constant as this forest with its mist and fog
I still can't see my way clear of.

Bloodroot

I.

He has rolled away from me
in sleep, though the heat still moves
between our bodies. His skin
will keep this flush for hours.
I have watched it before, this slow
fade of color, like the last bit of anger
giving back the tempered flesh.

My forefinger against his wide,
Slavic cheek, eyes moving beneath lids,
his mouth drops open slightly, closes
again. I want to put my hand there,
his mouth, keep it from rolling angry
words into the next tirade when this flush
has gone and we are again only
two people at odds over every thing
but this heat between us.

A red welt beneath his ear,
where, at the curve of neck,
I have marked him, and I cannot
recall how much of that was passion,
how much anger. I touch my lips
to that spot, feel the blood beneath raised skin,
the heat of it. His breath catches.

II.

Grandma called it *sweet slumber*, that juice
she squeezed from stem to drop onto sugar cubes,
slip into our mouths to quell a hard cough.

Sanguinaria.

Bloodroot.

Reddish-orange fluid leaked
from broken stems that looked for all the world
like bleeding, thin fingers;
crooked, bent, pointing.

III.

As a child, I took the dare of older cousins,
broke the root, tore stem from scalloped leaves,
white, star-like blossoms, touched
seeping red to the tip of my tongue.

There are things in the forest
that will kill you with ease,
give you only the slightest, tart
warning of toxin and I was sure,
in that moment when my tongue pulled back
and I spit, hunkered close to ground,
that this root was the end of me.
Wrong season, too close to the last frost,
maybe. You could eat a plant ten different ways
without harm, but eat it once
in early season, once
with the wrong time budding
and it might take your breath from you,
your sight, the feeling in your hands and feet.

I rolled against crunching leaves on the slope
of mountain, spitting wildly, vaguely aware
that Grandma had come to the commotion,

taken the root from the boys,
laughed.

When she lifted me to her shoulder
and said, *They's a reason I cut it with sugar,*

I relaxed into the ease of her voice, the sway
as she shifted her weight one leg to the other.

IV.

He turns his head toward me now,
eyes opening. I want to remember them
like this – brown as chicory and soft
with sleep, without question.
I take my fill quickly, memorize
flecks of gold and green in dark brown,

roll away from him, close my eyes,
and think of that day on the mountain –
Grandma balancing me on the point of her hip,
lifting my face to whisper,
Never take nothing to your mouth you ain't tamed yet.

What Passes For Conversation

I am on a cell phone given to me
by the attorney I work for.
I suspect she is trying to modernize me,
though surely she tires of my questions,
how do I listen to a message?
how do I delete it?

In twelve weeks, they will take
your breast. You say you are glad
to be rid of it, cancerous thing,
taker of hair and comfort and, maybe,
life. You say this without venom.

I tell you it's cold here, prematurely cold.
I am wearing two sweaters, one black,
one lime green, and a leather jacket
and I am still cold and isn't it still
September? *I don't understand this,*
I tell you. You say, *It's cold here, too.*

You say, *Wax poetic.*
I tell you, *Listen to the wind*
and I hold my phone away
from my face, into the strong easterly.
I hear you yell, *Tell me something beautiful*
and the phone is plastic and hard
and cold against my ear.
I say, *The fieldgrass is bent low,*
blades like crystal in this morning sunlight
with frost that hasn't yet disappeared.

Seduction, Like a Falling Back

I am guilty of wanting his body
evicted of mine, afterward, after
bodies have slowed, wanting his weight
off of me, the heat of his skin.

I am guilty this night of feigning sleep
to roll to my own corner of bed, sheets cool
and untouched and apart.

Too soon, I feel his breath against my shoulder,
the heavy weight of his head when he lays it
across my back, curling to me
like a child, long legs drawn up against mine.

I drag slow breaths and wonder if he knows
I only closed my eyes to avoid
talk, heavy and weighted beyond what I want
in the sated coming-down of muscle and mind.

I am guilty of starting this seduction tonight,
of reaching and pulling, tired of the sullen looks,
the aggravation I know he is entitled to.

I am guilty of needing to see the anger and hurt
go out of him like so much breath
held to bursting.

I will not lie and say I didn't enjoy it.

We are nothing to each other if not thorough.
This knowledge of body, places gone taut
with nerves and flush with blood raging
has always been at the base of this.

When he said to me, breath catching,
We are so good together, I heard myself
saying *Yes,* and wanting to stop myself
and knowing it was true,

if only in the way our bodies moved
for so many minutes harmonized, the pitch
and ascent of breath gone tangled, voices rising
counterpoint and hurried.

I feel the weight of him shifting,
sticky peeling of his arm from my back.
There is a part of me that wants to roll to him,
as if suddenly wakened, and take him against me.

When I hear the shower water running, I turn,
roll over to his pillow, pull the musky scent,
slightly cologned, against my face, imagine
missing him, imagine clinging to this pillow

for comfort the way I see him hesitate over mine
some mornings when he stretches his long body out,
diagonal to the bed, his head resting where mine
lay all night.

I half expect to see him catch me in this act,
his head suddenly poking from the bathroom,
as if this was a game,
as if this was anything
he could win.

The Shape of Me

Is Granddaddy's hands, long-fingered,
agile whittler, plucker of things better left
unseated. Sway of my mother's hips,
jitterbugging their way around the house,
cleaning, purging, so many things to dance
away. The sound of me, shifting
against the stone at my base, turn
of tongue to what is Southern
and mountain and all that my mother
erased from her careful mouth. My hair,
black as those Cherokee women's in the monochrome
pictures, nameless aunts and grandmothers,
something they didn't speak about
back then. The white is easiest;
the Irish smooth, freckled for character,
hazel eyes like indecision – not green
as those County Kerry hills, not brown
as those forgotten women in the margins
of our family bible. My body, curved
and swollen in the places of my mother,
grandmothers, places I force tight, taut to submission,
make my own against that presence in my bones
that says: At the base of it, you are
these people. At the base of it,
you are corn and tobacco,
Irish whiskey and coal dust,
sewn of the same frayed thread
and in the same ways,
loosely sewn.

Family Reunion

We crossed the plywood bridge – rotting,
rain-soaked, laid haphazard across a sinkhole
where the mines puckered the ground.
At the door to our great-grandfather's house,
we stopped to survey the wreckage. They said
he'd become a pyromaniac after that last stroke –
the one that left him calling us *boy* or *girl*,
our names and faces lost to him.

Ryan said, *This ain't Grandpa's house*
but I knew it was and pointed out the blackened
horseshoe hanging cockeyed to the door, the nail
missing, clinging to the frame like magic.
That's his horseshoe off the old milkwagon horse.
I'd seen pictures of this house in Grandma's album
marked *Mommy & Daddy* across the front.

Deep in forest overgrown and untended we stood,
a passel of great-grandchildren before the char.
We could still hear the high mandolin, the harmonized
singing of the adults on the other side of the forest, just
across the hill at Aunt Pinkie's house. Ryan said,
We ain't supposed to be here, but Johnny pushed past,
shouldered the door open, left us all choking on
the rot of 10 years' abandon, the smell of things
long gone.

We walked into the slant-walled room, all four walls
buckling, sagging, leaving large spaces
between roof and wall – enough that sunlight
from between the trees broke straight, thin lines
through the air, heavy now with dust and ash,
and seeing nothing there for us, no exciting secrets,
just old tins of cherry cigarettes and cans of lard,
we pushed each other back toward the door, leaving
a shuffle of footprints in the ash, everything else
as we found it.

Roadin'

I may try my whole life for that peace I can remember,
the comfort of body and ease of mind that drew everything
to a barely discernible hum as we lay stretched out, a clutch
of cousins, head to toe along the grass that stayed soft beneath
the shade of pinoak, the way my chest felt full, barreled
out with deep breaths of September air, contentment that came
with sun-dropped backfields and days moved into evening
like natural conclusions and

I am close to that feeling even now, in the gloaming,
when humidity thins to nothing
and the day's noise is left to a steady building
of cricket scratches and toad calls and I search
these back country roads, crunch and shot of gravel
beneath my tires, high lonesome tenors singing
mountain standards and I recall those evenings

Granddaddy loaded us
into the bed of the truck, drove
the old roads, rattle of cattleguards and dirt road dust
swirling behind us, looking to spot deer,
fox, an unusual tree or hawk streaking the field.

I am close to that grace when I remember
his face in the sideview mirror, always
glancing back, smiling at the sight
of his grandbabies; windblown,
brown-skinned, bellies full
with Grandma's pan-brown potatoes,
fried chicken and garden corn.
He saw it in us, that look of good breeze,
warm skin and full bodies, and

I wonder now if he was looking for it, too,
looking for that thing that would leave him
sated. Or maybe that was it for him,
that backward glance to us.

Beyond

I want to resent it –
that I'm back here again,
another Saturday
in a field by myself,
Grandma in the house,
cooking bacon, slicing tomatoes.

I want to believe there's more to it,
my life, than the repetition
of my Saturdays spent jostling
the tractor over hard ruts
where watermelon rows
used to line the ground, where
the boys, my cousins, tore rocks out,
tossing them to the woods, clearing
the way for tiller and seed.

I want to say I hate this intrusion
on my time, time I could be spending
reading books, walking the halls
of the Met or the Corcoran Museum.

But, after the first hour,
I am beyond the tingling and numbness
of legs gone overstimulated
with vibration and harsh sun,
beyond thinking of what lies past
the edges of field and trees.

There is no driveway in the distance.
There is no road leading away.
There is nothing beyond this pasture.
I am straddling the concentric circles
where the tall, untouched grass meets
the heap I have made beside it

and there is only the knowledge,
slow and precise,
that I will bring it all down.

Drought
New York City

Water shortage, again, we are destined
for short showers and brown grass in a drought
that seems to me displaced in a city – no crops
to wither, tomatoes gone puckered and new potatoes
hard as coal. City landscape is a different breed
of scorch, not so laughable as I imagined, learning
not to scoff as I stand at the great fountain before
Lincoln Center, empty of water, a thousand exposed
pieces of copper, drying and dull in the uncovered blaze.

Sycamores

Manhattan, September 12, 2001

Central Park, so oddly quiet, no people
walking, finches, even, subdued in their calls.
I find the trees, London Plantains, so much like
my sycamores back home, their mottled, bleached
bark, peeling like something burned
or shedding itself into something new.
My granddaddy's voice in my head, deep and calm,
When you're bad lost in the forest, find you a sycamore,
look as long as you have to cause they'll always be near
water you can follow out. They's no such thing as
completely lost;
just got to know what to look for to get you home.
I step over the small metal cage at its base, lean
my forehead against a smooth spot, soft as shellac, breathe
the musty familiar, close my eyes.
There is no smoke.
There are no buildings tall as the sky.
Only this tree, my fingers pulling against flaking bark,
pressing
my body flush against it until there is nothing to feel
but the bite and scratch, the worn, smooth
salvation of it.

Manhattan

for Darnell

City
that never sleeps;
we are somnambulant,
wandering the smoke and stench still
heavy

on us.
There are no more
cellos in the subway;
no balm of Saint-Saens, Debussy.
These are

the days
of Dvorak,
doublebass, low and dark,
dirge for what we cannot bury
or look

away
from. There is no
symphony at all now.
Musicians have closed their windows,
pulled down

the shades,
left us these streets
with no melody but
the flutter and rustle of the
missing

posters,
whipped by the wind,
tape pulling from edges
of lampposts covered in these lost
faces.

Last And Final Psalm

All those years of your warning voice calling to me,
Don't get so far from your roots that you can't feel them,
like some last and final psalm,
something breathed at me in the end
from lungs laced thick and hard with work
and coal's remnants – an arch of dust
I could almost see in puffs between us.

I am here in this city, brushing ash from my eyes,
near the place you said was unnatural, too close
to sun and clouds and air gone thin with height.
Walking with other medics to the site,
it's you I think of when I cough hard to bring up the dust,
think about men you dug from rubble of coal and slate,
things unwhole and crushed.

I remember the birds mostly, pigeons and grackles,
their wings cock-eyed, dusted dull gray
with ash we walked through,
and their eyes wide with cognizance,
as if they knew they had flown too close
or too far from where they nested.

Back Home After September

Open fields of dried,
winter-sapped brown moving past
the window I crack
for the rush of familiar,
cold air, scentless, icy-fresh.

Nearing Neavil's Mill,
trees become thicker, bending
sycamores against
Cedar Creek's edge, looming pines
that cup the woodthrush nests like

hands ready for some
offering. I stop midway
on the bridge, look down
onto first webs of ice skims,
reaching out from jutting banks

like tendrils of hair
on the water, hanging on
by God knows what. This
is home, safe, water with its
hold of rushing trout unchanged,

still worthy of time
spent stopped on a bridge. I am
embarrassed by tears
that come hard, unrelenting,
by the woman who sees me,

stops alongside me,
asks if I need help. I see
my breath before me,
icy marker hanging there,
falling to the ice below.

My voice comes softly,
the only words I can find
– *I am beholden* –
to this woman, to this place,
whoever might be listening.

All the Flying Things

I.

Getting chased by some number six
lead shot, for example, will move a crow
with speed that should scare you. Call them
bad omen, call them scraggly, flea-ridden,
but they twist the air to their fitting, fly
so close to you that you can smell the must,
ammonia-tinted and undercarriage-like.

II.

As kids, my friends and I ran panic-legged from bats –
dive-bomb at dusk, the chance they might
accidentally tangle in hair, flail
with sharp shrieks and feet
with no choice but to hold what bound them.

III.

Southern girl gone to Manhattan,
city of pigeons, crooked, gray ones, speckled
white and brown, cockeyed, one foot curled all wrong,
groups of them that crowded the sidewalks
for pieces of soft pretzel,
waterdogs, buns fallen through the metal diamonds
of trash cans.

IV.

I arrived just in time to see the towers fall, so much paper
and dust that for days twisted through the air in lieu
of birds. I found whole only the bodies
of pigeons and grackles, their dusty wings pitched
above their heads, orange eyes half-closed as if
squinting into the ash.

V.

They are here for my return, first day back,
city-weary on the backporch in Virginia, good
country air and sunslant through the poplars.
Dad has left a beige sheet on the back of my chair
to keep the mosquitoes off. I pull it up
to my neck, hear the claw-scratch
on the pressed wood of rail,
open my eyes to two crows balanced and staring,
hopping slightly, wing-flap more for show
than flight, before they perch the hickory in front of me,
so close I feel the air move with the flick
of oily feathers, see the way each toe curls,
spreads again, digs the easy flesh of limb.

VI.

They stare at me, unbound by etiquette.
If they could, these crows,
they might laugh or dig beaks to my flesh.

I know nothing of omens now.
These birds are familiar, their eyes are unchanged,
never blank. They watch me
until I close my eyes again, and maybe still
while I sleep.

Return

This is home:
overhang of poplars and oaks
where we climbed and ran, snuck cigarettes
and hid them beneath the lush bend of forest ferns,
where we took boys and kissed them until
our jaws ached, rode our bikes past worn trails
to the water tower where we dared each other
one rung higher, ran from packs of wild dogs, and later
sat at the top of the tower, holding hands, making out,
drinking strawberry Boones and wondering what the hell
there was to do in this town.

I made Manhattan home for long enough
to love the city and its noise, the Puerto Rican women
on 96th and Broadway who took my 50 cents, gave me
a Dixie cup of coconut gelado and smiled with gold teeth
like my Grandma's, the smell of heavy yeast and garlic
from H&H Bagels just beneath my gym, the mantra
of the old black man on 104th who called *Jesus! Jesus!*
as if calling him home to dinner.

I made Manhattan home for long enough
to break my heart when the towers fell,
when I trudged through ash with other medics
and stood helpless as all the rest
when they brought us no one.
I stayed long enough to hand a fine man my heart
and have him hand it back, long enough
to pine for fresh air and familiar sounds,
to pack my bags when my bank account emptied
for the hundredth time and my family beckoned.

Now I sit in this driveway, engine off, windows down,
alone until they realize I'm here, run out to greet me.

It has been a summer of heavy rains and already
mosquitoes and horseflies buzz my car, a dove
bends its awkward neck to sip from the standing water
between two hickories, daddy-longlegs are stretched
into corners of the garage, motionless in this heat.
The fields will have to be bush-hogged – too tall
for mowing, too full of thick weed and goldenrod.
It is all overgrown, perfectly entangled.

I Mark This Gone Place With Foxfire

Buchanan Co., VA

At the edge of coal country
I pull the car onto a switchback,
stop where road and hollyhock run together
where used to you could go this road
to the top of Drill Mountain.
I abandon the car to this unkept place,
walk between overgrowth of briar and honeysuckle vine,
walk until I find the crevice – large enough
to walk into – where Granddaddy hid blackberry brandy.
But I am too long in the city, too afraid
of fast-moving critters who covet these dark niches,
I reach in with only my leg, toes pointed,
sweeping the floor for that bottle.

I come away with nothing, gone
as the road we used to drive together,
gone as these mountains, peaks missing, lopped off
by draglines that decapitate it all, leave
this strange, foreign landscape, absent
the rush of the Dismal River, even the creeks dried up,
or gone underground.

I find a poplar stump, sit against its damp wood,
breathe deep and imagine apple blossoms,
patches of pennyroyal, hillsides unvanished.
This place gave you love and children, mandolin
and shaped-note singing, a taste for squirrel gravy
and fried bluegill, and those black lungs
that finally slowed you to a stop.

I stand and dig up the forest floor with the toes of my boots,
break this rotting poplar up with my heels, push it in chunks
beneath the ground, cover it over again. You taught
me this trick. You said,

I know this to be true: sometimes
when you bring up things, rot and all,
you get a queer thing of light,
glowing even as it dies.

afterword

Mountain women carry the earth close to their bodies, Lisa Parker declares in her long-awaited first book, *This Gone Place*. She explains, "I come from the spirit of a hundred women / who inhabit me, who are with me / in these cities, in these universities, / and who sing beneath my skin…." but this poet knows that her singing carries with it the often painful contradictions of a southern Appalachian upbringing. Carrying the earth close to our bodies doesn't compute well in our current culture, does it? And yet, the roots and sod of our place will save us, if anything will. Our poets have always known this.

I read this manuscript in its earlier version years ago after meeting Lisa at Hindman Settlement School. I thought it one of the finest first collections I'd seen. Over the next few years I watched lesser books find their way into print and celebration. Where was Lisa's book, with its powerful voices springing up out of the places that bred her? Here it is, now, and the long wait has worked its clarifying, mysterious work, giving us a book that resonates long after you close the covers.

In "Dreaming Grandaddy," the poet says, "lately, I've dreamed you / as part of the mountains – all six feet of you / stuffed into a coal seam." This poet has dreamed her poems into those same seams, into the switchbacks and laurel, the bodies of kinfolk gone, places that survive now only in the lines of her memorable poems.

Kathryn Stripling Byer

acknowledgments

I am grateful for the teachers in my life who gave me a love of words, especially Arlene Lofdahl, Annie McKenzie, and Jane Shipman. I am also especially grateful for a generous grant from the Money For Women/Barbara Deming Memorial Fund.

I am sincerely thankful for the gems I found at Penn State in Charlotte Holmes, Jim Brasfield, Sara Greenslit, Kim Thorsen, Kris Hudak, Suzanne Meth, and my soul sisters Robin Puskas and Lyrae VanClief-Stefanon who have known every version of every poem I've ever written and act as my literary compass. For my Appalachian writing family, my home at Hindman Settlement School, you good people are my touchstone, my connection to my culture, and my privilege to call found family. Though too many to name here, my special thanks to Jane Hicks, Leatha Kendrick, Mary Hodges, Jason Howard, and my big brother Silas House whose letters and music compilations have made my life fuller. Thanks, too, to Lee and Hal for sharing their cabin at MerleFest each year, making me laugh until my sides hurt, and letting Rae and me pick and sing all night long.

For my friends in the DoD, you have enriched my life and my writing in truly unexpected ways. TK, Elida, Stubby, Barry, JtB, Kevin, Galvan, and Nikki, thank you for the laughter and the education. Butch and Eric, there's nothing like roadin' with you guys, music turned up and windows rolled down. My Manhattan family, you made being creative a true art form and I'm so grateful for your support and love.

Brian, your talent stuns me and I'm blessed to know you. James, thank you for lending your talent to this book and your sweet smile to this process.

Finally, to my big, wonderfully crazy family, I am supremely blessed to have grown up in your company. Thanks to my cousins who have always been right there beside me and who tell the best stories. Thanks to my mother who has the gentlest soul of anyone I know and still believes I walk on water, my father who carried my poetry around in his briefcase and who taught me the serenity of a day on the pond, and my sister Laura who is my heart. Thanks also to Jackson and Peyton who remind me what it is to marvel at the small things. Most of all, this book wouldn't exist without my grandparents, Clyde and Fay Whitt, who gave me love and lessons and all the hard, beautiful truth of being Appalachian.

– LJP

about the poet

LISA J. PARKER is a writer, musician and photographer born and raised in Fauquier County, Virginia. She received an MFA in Creative Writing from Penn State in 1998 and has published in numerous literary magazines, journals and anthologies. She is the recipient of several writing awards including the Randall Jarrell Prize In Poetry, the National Allen Tate Memorial Prize In Poetry, and an Academy of American Poets Prize. Her photography was exhibited in New York City, where she lived for several years, as part of New York Public Library's *Storylines Project*. She currently lives in Virginia where she works in the Defense and Intel sector and continues to work on writing and photography projects. Her work can be seen at www.wheatpark.com.

CPSIA information can be obtained at www.ICGtesting.com
Printed in the USA
LVOW131834090613

337663LV00001B/2/P

9 781934 894293